I MUST
BELONG
SOMEWHERE

ALSO BY DAWN LANUZA

I MUST BELONG SOMEWHERE

DAWN LANUZA

Andrews McMeel
PUBLISHING®

ease my pains and impatience by reading

TRIGGER WARNING:

This book contains discussions on death, suicide ideation, violence, bullying, injury, self-harm, body image, sexism, and mental health. If you feel triggered in between these pages, feel free to give yourself the space and time to breathe.

Take care of yourself.

1

She didn't know where she was from.

On the first day of school, freshman year, people tried to know each other by asking three things: name, major, hometown.

She knew the answers to the first two questions, but she'd always answered the last one with a question mark. It wasn't that she lied; it was true. She had lived in that place longer than any place she'd been in, and yet she refused to call it home. She still thought of it as temporary, and she'd struggled to understand why, but then

she remembered.

She once slept in another city
and woke up in this town.
She'd never seen so much land
and trees and rocks and colorful flowers
bunched up in little bouquets of
yellow and pink, yellow and pink.
She was happy for a minute.

She thought she'd stumbled upon
a place where fairies could exist.
The fireflies haloed the top of her head,
crowned her their princess,
and granted her a wish.
She was who they'd been waiting for,
and if she opened her hands,
a glow would reveal her power:
a light, blinding and searing.

That summer, she played to her heart's content. She ran around the railways and let the dust kiss her feet as she danced and twirled around it. She picked fruits from her uncle's backyard and ate them until her chin was sticky from the nectar that dripped from her mouth. She convinced herself that she lived in a storybook because, for the first time, she was allowed to dip into a pool of water so cold her insides shivered. She loved her freedom, and she cruised the rivers looking for snails and toads, dared to visit the places where they said mythical creatures roamed.

And yet.

She knew that summer was ending. She started noticing notebooks piling up for school. The spiral spring had been taken off its sides, and the elders spun colorful yarns around to keep the leaves bound together. They started to bring up June, and it sounded like a threat, another separation from a world she just met.

But the day came when she had to leave. They had her bags packed and everything. They never said she was going home; she would just have to go. And because she was young and braver then, she asked the question no one had been asking.

She asked, "When are we going home?"

And she knew, the moment those words left her mouth, that she wasn't.

She's been leaving and arriving at places with a cautious heart since then. She's aware that living in places is temporary, but sometimes she allows herself to be caught up in the magic. Like that summer. With the breeze running its fingers through her hair, whispering promises to her ears as the sun kissed her cheeks to say, "Aren't you glad you're here?"

She convinced herself that wherever she is, she can build a home. But at times, she catches herself asking, *What is a home?* Did she forget what it was? Did she ever even learn what it should feel like?

Our vibe vibrant
That's the vibe

2

Every once in a while she is convinced that she doesn't belong
here anymore.
Yet she doesn't know where she should be just yet.
She finds herself where she is because she doesn't know where
else to be.

Where would you go? she asks herself. *If everything would
be taken care of, where would you rather be?*
But she can't see it that way yet.

Her mind carries all of the worry and the weight.
Sometimes, when she's in a new place, wandering and
learning its streets, she just hears herself sighing, *I must
belong somewhere.*

She hasn't found it yet,
but she hasn't given up on the idea of it.

3

I am a suitcase:
holding these things together,
keeping them inside.

see the woe
believe them

4

I have been walking around your town,
tiptoeing, in case you're around.
Then I realized:
you do not own these streets.

Nobody put a claim on
which ends we should
or shouldn't be.

You are merely living,
and so am I.

So *am I*.

walking around
the town, where you
built your own
family for
so many yrs.
it was extremely
lonely
you have no idea
I have no idea
why? what are
the lessons?

5

The thought of being in the same place as you scares me, but staying away from you for too long scares me in a different way.

6
—

She doesn't have a bucket list.
Thinking about it felt like
enumerating things
until she's ready to die.

That day, when she
boarded that plane,
sat one row behind
the emergency exit,
she thought,
If this is my last day,
I wouldn't mind.

She didn't like to admit it,
but she feared death
when she was a child.
Now she found herself
actually thinking,
It could be any time now.

She used to worry about the things she'd leave:
the mess they would have to clean up for her,
the secrets they'd reveal at her funeral,
the things she didn't admit for various reasons.

But she's started talking now.
She's doled out apologies
to the people who need them.
She doesn't sleep with the thought of
making it better next time.

She tries to make it better *now*.

And if it doesn't work that way,
she lets it go.
She knows now that she can only do
what she can at the time.
She doesn't waste her energy on someone
who won't—*can't*—reciprocate her love.

She doesn't live with regrets now.
And if she leaves this earth,
she will.

She's free from herself now.

7

Freedom is looking at your things and thinking, *I don't need all of this.*

- looking for my own feelings in those pages.
- I do not want to feel it all by myself or it just is me feeling all of these.
- I want my people and I want my safe place peace

8

In the winter,
the skies are bland
and turn the city gray,
but there are nooks and crannies
in between the alleyways.

There's a tiny bookshop
with pocket-sized stories
and a chocolatier
with his chocolate-covered cherries.
A café that was named after a cat
that makes the perfect cup
and a bench in the middle
in case one needs to stop.

When you reach that corner,
remember to look up.
You'll find that somebody
drew you a heart.

— *graffiti*

9

He asked her,
"Why do you keep writing love poems?
There are so many things
in the world that need
to be discussed:

poverty and war,
deceit and injustice."

And she said,
"What hurt could
a little love poem do?

Every day that we see
the world crumble,
how are we not able
to remember:
a little bit of love
could make this better."

losing you, to keep
my hope in love

eventhough its so little like a grain of
rice left after you
To me, its enough.

10

There are streets that stay alive in your head.
Like St. Kilda and that busy street of
bakeries,
window displays of sweets and
live music blasting in your ears.
People from all over the world
speaking in their native tongues,
clinking beer bottles as the sun
melts into creamy clouds.
It's orange and pink,
violet hues;
neons, sharp strokes,
alleys, and walls.
Posters of people
writing poetry with their hands.
It's everyone speaking out at once:
a harmonious cacophony
of lives being lived
that summer day.

11

Her mind is a born voyager,
always curious about what's to discover,
willing to embark on expeditions
to locate the unknown.

Her heart, however, is a creature of habit.
It is craving the sunlit porch,
the hot pot of chamomile tea,
a worn-out winter blanket.

She flees because
she can't help but sate
her interest,
but she always comes back
home to the familiar.

She allows herself to be called
a wanderer,
but she always knew that her
goal was to settle:
to find herself satisfied,
to no longer wonder
what was missing
from her life.

12

They tried so hard to build a home.
There's a roof above their heads,
but they're still seeking shelter.

Did they really have the time
and space to recover?

13

She wasn't one of the kids who wanted
her parents to get back together.
There was no together,
even before.
She saw how her mother blossomed
after they left him,
and she would rather have that
than recall her silence
in his presence.

She learned how to choose herself by her mother's example.

Not everyone would understand it;
she remembered people looking at her
strangely whenever she said,
"No, I don't want my father home."

For some people, that made her seem bad,
like she was the devil child,
but she always knew:

you can't repair something that never worked,
and that was the truth.

14

As she made her way onto
the Great Ocean Road,
they talked about forest fires
and how people learned
to build their homes
with protection in mind,
in case the fires started.

They will;
it's just a matter of time.

On her left stood trees
with no sign of life,
trunks black as charcoal,
branches spread out.
Standing tall
above the wreckage of it all.

And she'd never felt so proud.

15

A screaming match in the kitchen. They should have
christened this new home with kind words and hushed tones.

For even the most loving words won't sound very loving in a
harsh and raised voice.

16

It's one thing to be a spectator of someone else's loneliness, another thing to be a prisoner of your own.

17

I've never read your suicide letters,
never seen them either.
I know that they're there,
tucked between the bed
and your pillows.
Maybe they'll slip out of
your books or sketch pads.

But I do know this much:
you've had the words
written on your face
all along.

I read them from the way you recoil,
body curled into a tight ball.
You never turn your lights on,
the darkness a blanket as you shiver.
You remain quiet during the day
but a noise of pots and cutlery
during the night.

I've never read
your suicide letters.

I've lived with them instead.

18

People started to disappear.
We'd always heard of this,
but it was a different time—
that is, until the names
of the missing sounded familiar.

Like Joni, who I grew up with,
lived next door,
played with my brother after school.
They said he was one of them, too.

He used to walk around the corridors,
wore shirts that were washed and ironed.
He was nicer than most,
didn't care if someone was cool.
He taught me how to jiggy that one time
'cause my limbs didn't know.
He said, "Just bend your knees,
move to the beat."

But that was then.
We had lives outside,
grew up.

He slipped out one night,
only to be taken in
as an exchange
for someone.

Caught, red-handed.
He ran through the streets
carrying packets.
Door-to-door deliveries,
cloaked by darkness.

I didn't know how he
had gotten into this.

He was the boy I knew,
led the prayers when we were both in
Catholic school.
He always had a pretty smile.
That's what I remembered
to be true.

People started to disappear
long before I even noticed.
They skipped towns.
They lay low.

The unfortunate ones got caught.
The lucky ones chanced upon redemption.
The poor ones were found on the road.
Sometimes wrapped up like animals,
others left to bleed on the very streets
they grew up in,
in front of the people
they grew up with.

People disappeared all the time,
but now we feel them missing.
They warned us about this,
and yet we just keep watching.

19

You also disappeared, didn't you?
You ran to a far enough place
to avoid what was happening to you
and everyone you knew.

But even with the distance, you learned:
no amount of miles could make you
any less
frightened.

There's a scribble
at the bottom of a page
of your old notebook.

Once you were afraid, too.
Someone once told you:

whatever it is that scares you,
do that.

20

Year twenty-nine was
learning to say yes,
knowing when to say no.

Finding a place,
a familiar face,
having the courage to go.

21

Half of me is worried about the lives I'm not living;
half of me is too tired to do anything about it.

22

How hard is it to leave someone,
wondering if you'll come back home
to a corpse?

You either choose to stay
or leave so fast,
so far away, that

you won't have to see
the blood trail,
hear the last hitching breath,
smell the stink of a day-old body,
taste the chill of their stiff fingers
where there is no pulse,
no blood,
no life,
no recognition of the man
you loved.

How do you carry
the guilt of leaving
for a moment
for yourself?

How hard is it
to live with someone
who wants to die,
knowing they want to live
but somehow can't quite make it?

It's like standing over a cliff,
your hand stretched out,
hearing yourself yell, "Take it!"
You see it in their eyes.
They want it.

You hold on and pull them up,
but the weight, even for you,
is too much.

You strain your muscles—
no, don't let go.
You get that resigned look,
and you know.

They will let you go—
and soon.

23

She's traveled so much the past year,
but she's barely heard the words:
"Should the cabin lose pressure,
oxygen masks will drop from the overhead area.
Please place the mask over your mouth and nose
before assisting others."

He had been so willing to die,
and she had been so willing to save him.

24

I must find a way
to still choose myself despite
holding on to you.

25

When I was young, I learned about a man named Ettore Majorana, who chose to disappear. He was young and very smart, but one day, he bought a ticket to Naples, got on the boat, and never returned. He left a note to his friends to apologize for his absence, then sent a telegram to cancel all of his commitments.

There were several hypotheses regarding his disappearance, including suicide, but I always believed that he was alive. I chose to believe that he was one of the few ones who managed to vanish, chose to build his life the way he wanted it.

I never forgot about Ettore. I had him in the back of my mind, pictured him living his best life, far different from the one he left behind.

Recently, I decided to type his name in the search box and learned that his case of disappearance had been closed. Someone witnessed him in Buenos Aires, doing god knows what, but I smiled at that.

As I sit here with my glass of wine, I make a toast:

to Ettore,
who disappeared—
but also
to the man he chose to be
and the life he must have fully lived.

26

Some things you love
won't always serve their purpose.

You have to let go.

27

I didn't want to
just survive this life.
I wanted to live.

28

I sat on Fed Square
as the sun set slow.
There were pigeons
trying to fight for a crumb
and a family of four.

I dared to ask,
"Can I actually live like this?"
And I meant: transient.

You sat next to me
and said, "Sure.
As long as you always
have a place to dock."

I've been away since;
I'm still wondering where that was.

29

On the train ride to the city, there was a boy who was
making kissing sounds with his girl. Every sentence would
end with a kiss. As an unwilling spectator, I started to wince,
but the truth is—

I remembered when your sentences all ended with your lips,
hitting the sides of my cheeks, my temples, my skin. I sat
there not knowing what to do with my hands, my chest, my
lungs, my fingertips.

I didn't know what to do with you, soaking my skin with
     your wet kisses and your love—
my love.
I didn't know what to do with your love.

I didn't know how to kiss you back, didn't know how to love
     you just as much when the truth is I do.
I do.

I just didn't know how to show you. I had to learn from years
     and years of replacement lovers, storybooks, and novels.
     Now I think I know.
Yet there is no you left to show.

30

She wanted to be alone,
but with someone.

That should make sense.

31

You stopped intruding on my dreams.
In fact, I am convinced:
you now live in my subconscious,

you little
castaway.

You start fires and let them
burn through the night.
You take from my land,
let your feet sink through
the mud.
You run mad,
leaving foot trails in the sand.
You throw spears,
climb trees.
You seek for sustenance,

you hungry
little thing.

You ignore my call
to make no sound.
You spell out capital
H - E - L - P
with seashells
and granite.

You captive,
you captivate me
still.

You show up every once in a while
to remind me of the promises
I broke,
the lives I could have hoped
to live, to make sure
I don't forget.

I've got you trapped
on a little island
for myself.

I am your shipwreck,
thunder and lightning.
I brought you here to abandon,
so you hunt me down
and haunt me for it.

32

The roaring twenties:
learning how to be alone,
wondering, *How long?*

33

You're a little too ashamed to admit that it's getting a little
   lonely.
Not all the time.
But some days, you feel the loneliness sneak up on you,
grazing your arms like a phantom limb,
pulling you in for a quick embrace
only to leave
as soon as your mind starts to wonder,
as soon as your heart whispers:
How long has it been?

34

I don't want
to be loved
in sample sizes anymore.

I wanna be ravished
whole.

35

Go ask the question:
how do you want to be loved?
Use it as a map.

— *What's your love language?*

36

I am always looking for places to go;
you liked staying in places,
setting down roots and so.

I grew wings,
but sometime in between,
I think I left my heart
where you've been.

I know where to return.
You're still there,
feet planted in the soil,
aren't you?

37

I loved the idea of you,
conjured from the pieces,
memories you left.

I made you human
in my head.
Living and breathing,
in my head.
Safe and stable,
in my head.
Loving me always,
in my head.

I loved the idea of you;
it was so convenient.

I made you as real
as I needed,
used you as a shield
from the rest.
The person I blamed
for failing to do
what I needed.

38

At ten, she staged a little coup.
She put up barricades
and staged being sick on
Friday afternoons.

She skipped school.

She didn't like how the girls started to change.
They stopped playing,
picked up combs,
stared at pocket mirrors,
and whispered about boys.

She didn't like how the boys kept bugging her.
They started sending her plastic roses,
passed her balled-up pieces of paper
containing meaningless words.
They never meant what they wrote.

She also didn't like to sweat
and how the sun hit her back
from where she sat in the afternoons.
She hated how she smelled.
It didn't belong to her.

She hated the hair growing in her armpits
and soon enough down there, too.
Her chest itched, and she'd been growing
here and there—
she hated it so much
that she staged a little coup.

Who cared about percentages
if she was wholly changing?
Her grades fell way back to the line of seven.
She still liked reading—
volunteered to recite stories—
but nobody would listen.

Her mother handed her a bra
and a deodorant stick.
She cut her hair right by her chin.

Over the holidays, she turned a year older.
She returned to school,
approached the circle:
girls with their detangling combs,
foldable mirrors,
floral handkerchiefs.

She came and told the story
of how she bled
the very first time.
She didn't like it, but somehow,
she thought,

I belong now.

39

She grew up in front of the TV
waiting for people to come home.
She made friends with fiction,
convinced herself that she had to be
one of them:
tall, white, blond, and blue eyed.
Everything she wasn't born to be:
petite, brown, black haired, and dark eyed
but—

She saw Cameron Diaz get married in this movie.
It happened hours before she had
a screaming match with this lady,
just two women fighting for
the same man.

The blond girl got the guy.
Didn't matter if there was
someone else who knew him better.
Didn't matter if there was
someone else who loved him longer.
The blond girl got the guy
because she was young,
and cute, and rich.

The girl who won was the crème brûlée,
and she was the Jell-O—
no, she was sticky rice
wrapped in banana leaves.
She had no idea what
Jell-O even was.

40

She dove into the classics,
found Ali MacGraw by the doorstep,
crying all alone.
She and Ryan O'Neal had been fighting,
so when he finally saw her,
he said, "Sorry."

And then the actress said the phrase that she had to repeat
over the years, hoping she could finally understand what it
meant.

Love means never having to say you're sorry.

More than a decade had passed, and she still let that play
    around her mouth,
like a tongue twister.
A riddle.

She still didn't get it.
"Sorry" is a nice word.
"Sorry" means feelings were considered.
"Sorry" means "I learned."
And love?

Love means having the courage to say you're sorry.

41

She's learning the word
"sorry."
She's always known it
but doesn't say it enough.

She would rather see people
walk out than say,
"I'm sorry;
I didn't mean that."

Because some days, she does.
She really means it to hurt.
She hurts before she gets hurt,
makes a habit of
swallowing a five-letter word.

She's been learning the word
"sorry."
She's always known it,
but she's been meaning it now.

42

All of her shoes were in the shade of brown.
She noticed this as she stared at her new shoes,
the ones he bought for her after they'd had lunch.

Lunch, his equivalent of cramming in
minutes, hours, days, weeks, months,
years of her life.
She forgot how frequently he'd come.

Such an effort to travel for two hours
to see her for small talk.
She forgot what they talked about,
but she remembered telling him,

"All of my shoes are in the shade of brown."
He told her that he was the same.
It was the only common thing they had,
apart from the DNA.

She was always looking for that,
for something to be shared,
apart from the nose she supposedly
inherited.

They had these one-hour Sundays,
but she still never knew him like that.
They never moved from the small talk;
she doubted he knew her that much.

He always missed her birthdays.
He got confused with the dates.
She didn't remind him.
Every year, she played the game of
"would he finally remember?"

It was funny at first,
an inside joke.
But as the years piled on,
she just started to roll her eyes
at the late text,
the generic greeting.

Meanwhile, her grandfather had nine kids,
and when she was cleaning out his things,
she saw a piece of paper with his scribbles:
all the names of his kids,
the dates of their birth—
she assumed so he would never
mix them up,
no matter how plenty
or how old they were.

God bless my grandfather—
she took a photo of his scribbles
and posted it online.
He did it right.

Through the years, she'd said,
"Doesn't matter, he tried."
But she is so
tired.

Sometimes she just needed it to be done right.

43

The first time she held a boy's hand,
it became hot news.
She became an overnight sensation,
and if they had tabloids in school,
she'd be on the front page for sure.

The headlines would read,
"WHO IS SHE?"
They'd have her worst picture,
zoom her in like a criminal.
They knew exactly who she was.

She had always been around,
doing her own thing,
never really in the way of
couples; it wasn't her thing.
She didn't do relationships at
fifteen.
She had a dream:
she just wanted to sing.

They paired her up with a boy.
Everyone liked him,
but she didn't know just how much
until she decided
maybe
she could be his.

He didn't seem to disagree.
There were ten fingers,
two hands,
two arms linked,
and it was done
with an understanding,

"You and me,
we're a thing."

But then they weren't.

For he was everybody's,
and she was a nobody.

Until she became their target.

She wasn't ready for it.
She became the fool
who stormed through
the deluge.

He said he tried to protect her,
yet she was the only one
walking around with archers
aiming at her every move.

He said he still wanted her,
said it over and over
through the years,
but she refused.

He could spend all of his years
trying to prove it,
but she was not done
punishing him for what he did—
or didn't do.

He let go of her hand.
He watched her drown.
He didn't love her
the way she needed
to be loved.

44

She changed her name after they'd slandered it,
baptized herself with a word that alluded to light,
and what a name she chose,
because where she came from,
it was dark.

It was whispers in the corridor,
raised eyebrows,
laughter echoing on the marbled floors,
private messages asking,
"Is it true, what they are saying about you?"

But what is the truth?
Since changing her name, she's buried the memories of the
girl who went through the firing squad, the same one who
took the bullets to her back as she kept quiet about the
attacks.

Her new self got a new face to match. She's now all red
lipstick and charcoal eyeliner, no more baby powder, original
Chapstick.

She's a woman now.

The girl they talked about in harsh tones, she's gone now. She
got rid of the girl after the shooting. She took her body to the
woods and gagged her mouth with a piece of cloth. Not that
she would need it—the girl kept her mouth shut when she
was still alive, afraid of what her voice would sound like.

But she still put a finger over the girl's lips and shushed her. *Shhhhhh.*

She went to the river and called herself new, scrubbed off the drying blood from her skin, and warded off the ghost of the girl she once knew.

Before she closed the casket, she told the girl, "I would never be like you."

Never again.

She's got a new name. A new face. A new life. She's out here to get you.

45

Culprits don't deserve
recognition to make a point
about survival.

— Never thank them for your strength

46

We've come to the portion of the night where you slather yourself with the words "You're not good enough." You don't know where it came from. Earlier, you were sure you'd done things right, and you even came home satisfied, but somehow, at night, the words keep coming up. "You're not good enough." You manage to sleep through it, after fighting it off and your need to further self-destruct. Some days are just like this. You do well, and then you don't. You wake up like you've gone through a battle, and isn't it the truth? You wrestle with your doubts and sleep with the demon clutching at your heart, because tomorrow is another day to prove to yourself: *you are*.

47

Sadness comes home,
fixes himself a drink,
sits in my living room.

Sadness used to be a visitor;
I, a reluctant host.
A friend, an enemy,
sadness knows no boundaries.

Sadness wears a robe,
mocks me as I knew it all along.
Sadness never leaves.
Sadness is where I live.

Sadness welcomes me home,
motions me to close the door.
Sadness stays,
keeps me captive for days.

Sadness lives within.
Sadness is where I live.

48

We dress pain pretty,
package it nicely,
hand it over to your hands.

The truth is what you have
in your hands—
however rough,
however delicate—
is us.

In pieces,
vignettes.
With images
that we choose to reveal
as much as conceal.

Please take care of us.

49

She's been thinking about the dress she'd wear on her wedding day when she started wearing them. At fourteen, when she was asked to put makeup on. They shaved her eyebrows and painted her new ones.

It was the summer, which meant no school. No one would see how different she looked.

She grew.
She noticed.

There's a fully beaded gown waiting to hug her body; doesn't matter if they haven't been acquainted before. They were sure it would fit, because she is tiny, and at this age, she learned a dangerous lie that was passed on like it was the truth:

tiny is an easier fix than big.

At fourteen, she was pretty much skin and bones, but she had bumps where it mattered the most. The boys at school started talking about whose shirt buttons tended to pop open. She hated hearing them talk about it, how they forgot the fact that the girl had a face and a name. To them, she was just her breasts.

Yet she also found herself looking down, questioning her worth over a body part.

There were pins pricking her sides when they pulled the dress back. They sucked her in to make her look svelte and a whole lot more grown-up. Then again, Juliet married Romeo at this age. Maybe she wasn't that young.

She told them it hurt, and they tried to fix it, but it was still there. A phantom needle poking her when she took a breath. She said it's fine, anyway, 'cause what's a prick? What's a tiny needle going to do with the rest of her body?

And she didn't want to be known as the prickly one: difficult, complains a lot. 'Cause as much as everything in the room was overwhelming, she liked it.

She liked the rush.
She liked what she saw in the mirror, when they were done
     painting her face.
It didn't look quite like her,
but she could get used to it.

See, this girl,
She was beautiful.
Her skin was fair,
her hair was slick and tight,
her face

was not hers,
and yet
it was.

It was her
but tenfold.
Better.
Prettier.
Older.
Beautiful.

Not her.

She walked that runway with just the memory of the
     spotlight hitting her face. She saw spots as soon as she
     turned backstage, but
she was welcomed with compliments.

She felt good.
She looked good.
She was dressed like a woman about to get married.
She was gonna get her happy ending.

Since then she'd flipped through
bridal magazines,
deciding on a dress that would flair out
like gardens at her feet.

She told her sister about her dream,
but she was quick to see that
she only wanted a wedding.

She was too young then,
and she hadn't seen a marriage
that made her want it.

All she knew was a house
that was mostly empty.
Sundays obligatory.
No speaking.
Just talking out loud.

But she had a dream dress.
She dog-eared the page
as she let the book sit
on the coffee table.

Just in case she stumbled upon something wonderful.

50

Just how wonderful?
Nick Drake wrote about it once.
Play "Northern Sky" now.

51

Love came to her at sixteen,
too soon to be anything.
It was long walks
and midnight talks,
lying on the grass,
counting shooting stars,

but then nothing.

Love came to her at twenty-three,
too much to be taken in.
It was oceans and miles,
changing of seasons and
daylights,
being apart,

but then nothing.

Since then,
love hasn't come around.
If it does, may it be
the right one.

52

He won't come.
She's been waiting this long and for what? All he's sending
    are messages in bottles still floating in the ocean aimlessly.

He threw them out into the water a long time ago.
Somehow she's still waiting at the shore, watching the tide,
    hoping it brings her his words. But he won't come.

He has a boat, and he's been sailing through.
He could have just met you, but here she was, a deserted
    island.
Waiting for a drizzle.
Waiting for a word.
Waiting for his love.

53

You were the only one who believed that you kept your love
for him a secret. Everyone knew. You told them. You didn't
say the words, but you spoke about it in ways that would
have been understood by anyone. All this time you were
waiting for an answer, but it has been staring you in the face.
Years and years and still counting. How long will you keep
denying?

He doesn't love you.

If he did, you wouldn't be here waiting for a crumb to fall
off his mouth just to nourish you. How famished you are.
How malnourished you've been from choosing to love a man
who has not fed and will not feed you the kind of love that
you require.

You are this close to death for being stubborn.
Let yourself be carried out of his cradle,
be caressed by a hand
that won't rob you of hope.

Let yourself be loved, woman.

It has been too long.
Let yourself be found.
You have been missing
and missing out for so long.

54

Wind-up toy, how far?
His hands are on the winder,
testing your limits.

— *You're only without power if you let him take it*

55

What are we doing keeping trinkets of each other, collecting souvenirs of where the other has been? I sent you a postcard, and you pinned it to your corkboard. I wrote you your favorite poem from your favorite film. You played a song in your bedroom that reminded me of you, and you told me about it, too.

Sometimes I dream about getting these messages from you.

You used to give me your ticket stubs, and I've had them hidden somewhere in a pile of things that I've kept with every move. I've changed rooms and houses seven times since, but I always carry you.

And yet we revisit each other only like this.

Why can't we come home?
Why are we settling with pieces when we are parts of a
    whole?

56

Sometimes I dream about
full conversations,
but I wake up to
empty notifications.

I keep waiting for you
to show up,
but you never do.

I've got to stop waiting to hear back from you.

57

Troubled kid who sat in the back
always seemed to have his shirt untucked.
Their teacher scolded him for many reasons;
he was just all over his lessons.

Somehow she ended up sitting next to him.
He never looked up,
busy shading with his blue pencil,
flirting with shadows and light.

She started to watch his world
instead of the lessons she needed to learn.
One day, he finally handed her a pencil,
saved her a space to draw,
but she only wrote.

She wrote him letters;
he would write her back
in tiny, messy scribbles.
She talked in upside down alphabets
and forgot about graphs.
She gained a pen pal
without purchasing stamps.

That same year, her family
moved away from the city.
She could've sworn she wrote him once
on scented stationery.

She can't remember if he ever wrote back.
Seemed like he would,
but she wouldn't know.
It required postage and stamps.

58

Airplanes, cargo trucks,
my heart had been traveling
in tiny trinkets.

— *send to:*

59

Let it be a graze.
Our whole encounter was a series of them.
A day apart,
the next flight,
an early checkout—
if we met now, it would be unlike us.
We were always just seconds from being.
A spark,
never a flame.
Let it be a graze.

60

I love you loudly:
midnight scribbles, ink and keys,
words screaming on sheets.

61

You smell like summer.
Like the hallways at noon,
dashing to art class,
like youth.
Like the breeze touching the ends of my skirt,
like skipping, humming a tune.
You are green grass,
scent of the earth,
Hawaiian ginger,
bright yellow shirt.

You smell like a beginning;
oh, how I cherished you.

62

No love is wasted;
look how much I gained from it:
Poetry. Magic.

— *among other things*

63

Nobody said you wouldn't miss the very person you dismissed.

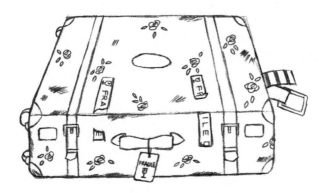

64

Remember that night?
You said,
"Come home with me tonight."
We walked under those streetlights,
hand in hand.

Years since,
I still keep going back
to that room,
in your bed—
it's all in my head.

This is where you last lived,
where it last felt like home.

This is where I belonged.

65

I am not honest.
I hold back words with my tongue.

Never with my hand.

66

I bought a house.
I got a car.
They said I had it made.

I went away
and stayed that way;
I'm just living in a suitcase.

Which goes to say:
life is not about how much we make;
it is what we make of it.

67

She lived for ten weeks with two weeks' worth of clothes and since then realized that she didn't need a lot to get by. She knew that she surrounded herself with things that she could live without, thinking that the more she acquired, the more reason she had to get by.

She could curate a museum called "things I shouldn't have bought and have no use for, but I got them anyway." She buys to exercise her need for control because she is, ironically, powerless over it.

When she lived in a suitcase, she started to count the things she *did* have.

She had her friend: living, breathing, twirling leftover spaghetti with her fork for breakfast.

She couldn't imagine what the world would be like without.

68

Your friends took photos.
You weren't in them at all.
Cruel reminder.

— *You left us awhile ago*

69

I've killed you
a thousand times
in my head.

I've often wondered
how you would do it.

Would you grab that knife
downstairs,
the one I used to cut up
apples and pears,
to slit your wrists open?

Would you drink a bunch
of pills,
pretend to sleep,
and never wake up?

I will never know
how you've designed
your own death.
I'm not waiting for you to do it.

I wish you'd completely forget
being the architect.
I wish you'd throw away your blueprints.

70

They have called her so many things,
but she is actually just a good actress.
She never is,
but she likes to pretend.
She sits and watches
and imitates
until she convinces one.

Sometimes all it takes is one for the rest to believe.

She plays a part
until a new role catches her eye.
She chases a new dream,
a new being.

She is never just one thing.
She is a collage of every being
that she has watched
and has taken from:

a strand of hair,
a drop of sweat,
a flake of skin.

She is a papier-mâché
of the people
she wants to be.
Somehow she expects
to find herself in a ball of
leftovers.

But who is she underneath it?
What is her true gift?

71

Doesn't matter what I do;
you still see me as a failure
for not being able to marry,
not bearing a child,
like I've got things mixed up
in my insides.

I know.

Despite my knowledge,
these words swirl around
my belly,
a fetus of doubt and worry,
a voice in the back of my head
saying my existence
depends only on my ability
to birth another life.

I'm sorry if I am not able
to love properly,
or in time,
at least according to your
time lines.

Maybe I have always been slow
or I just never could
or would get it at all.

But I am not sorry
for taking my time,
for weighing my options,
for choosing what I like.

72

These days, I feel like
my head is full but the rest
of me is empty.

— *peak anxiety*

no one knows
how much I cried
that day

73

She's tired of explaining how many times she's already injured her ankle. *Too many times.* The first time wasn't that bad. The last time lasted for months. Her leg atrophied, and she used crutches for the first time. She was stripped of her freedom, couldn't even bathe without a chair to sit on, couldn't even climb to her own room, couldn't even drive to places.

She's never felt so frustrated, telling herself every week that she'd be able to walk by this time, but days kept going, the calendar sheets flipping over.

She had so much planned, her little getaways. She wanted to wake up one day able to spring from the bed, but it never happened.

She was worried, but she was more anxious about the task of *not* letting the people around her worry. She missed going to events and places because she didn't want to keep telling people the story of how she hurt herself while wiping the cringes off their faces.

She remembered how she walked from where she fell to her hotel room. She held on to a girl she just met, and she kept telling her sorry. She didn't know why she was apologizing when it was an accident.

Women have to stop apologizing for things that are not their fault.

Past the one-month mark, she decided that she needed the healing to be sped up. She was sick of feeling helpless. She kept googling how long this would take and how severe it was. Her doctor just instructed her to attend seven sessions of therapy, but it still didn't get better, and it was too slow for her.

She understood that injuries could take a couple of months to heal, but she wanted to know how long she should nurse her broken heart.

When she heard her ankle land on the ground, it broke her heart.

It had been two years since she last fell from the stairs, and she wasn't able to walk for a month. They made her swear to never hurt herself again, but these were accidents, weren't they?

She sprained her ankle more than five times in this lifetime; she started dreaming about falling and waking up in terror from it. She breaks into a sweat every time she almost trips, has invested in footwear that won't risk her ability to get to places.

Her feet don't feel the same anymore, and she gets tired from standing too long, but in three months she's found herself walking again. She is still so afraid that she could make the wrong step and truly be unable to get up again.

She stares at the crutches she bought, knowing that they would have better use if she gave them away, but in the back of her mind there's a *just in case*.

She could barely remember the first time she injured her ankle. She reckoned she went to school and laughed off the incident, but since then she learned how fragile human bodies were.

She witnessed too many adults during physical therapy learning how to walk again. What a breeze it must have been for people when they were children. There were no voices in their heads telling them, *You used to do this. Why can't you just do it again? Hurry up.*

When she sat and watched, she learned that healing takes time. Learning how to do things again does, too. The struggle doesn't mean that she won't get there.

The misery is real, but so is the hope.

So is the hope.

74

"You should toughen up"
is why I'm hard on myself.
I've been told I'm soft.

— *like "soft" is a bad word*

75

I look forward to the day
I won't feel bad
just because somebody decided
I'm not good enough.

Im on that day
They dont know shit
Im good enough

76

Early riser,
the patriarch.
Roosters crowing
in the yard.

Fowls with
feathers black
and brown,
blue hiding just
underneath, a little peek.

Mornings smelled like
black coffee,
fog and dew,
a sliver of rust.
I bowed my head,
felt the weight of his hand.

Man of few words.

I counted the coins
from his little basin,
soggy orange bills
smelling like fish gone rotten.

I got sick:
no fever,
just nausea,
vomiting, and
a really bad feeling.

People started
smearing saliva
on my tummy
in case they were
the cause of what
I was feeling.

They called it *balis*.

I'd never felt like this
or even heard of it.
I supposed it was
one of those things,
like the *duwende* and
kapre; they'd already
warned me about it.

The next day
my grandfather drew
a small wet cross
on my skin.
I took another
nap, and then

I was all right,
back on my feet.
It was just like magic.

77

Once you learn the power of "not yet,"
you will feel a certain kind of ease.
It is not now,
but someday,
somehow,
through some way,
you will.

78

Some days feel like you've grown,
proud of the journey you took
and how far you've come.

Some days feel like none of it matters at all,
not until he's returned,
not until a second chance is earned.

Some days you're proud
of the person you're
becoming
Some days you cry for things
you left behind

79

You ask yourself how your very first session went. It went well. After, it was . . . well.

You feel awful. Like you have allowed someone to peek into your insides but not give you the response that you wanted. You feel angry for looking at a stranger's face while your eyes leaked. You wiped those tears, but the words echoed: "What are those tears for?" You feel small for being asked questions and for feeling forced to answer—because this was what you wanted, right? An honest conversation when all your life you felt as if you'd been excluded from it, protected by kind lies to garnish your life with confectionary. *Isn't life sweet?* But every once in a while your insides feel rotten. You sprinkle your life with sugar once more: you buy a hefty thing you show off as if to say, "Look at me. I've got all of this under control."

But as you sat there, you knew there was a rebellion going on inside of you. You sought counsel and landed in a room with a stranger who asked you, "What are you afraid of?" You were afraid of saying what they were. You tried to grasp a specific fear by its tail, but it was too fast to clear out, unwilling to be coaxed and spoken into presence, to be dealt with face-to-face to perish. You came up empty, looking like a fool who could not articulate what she needed to eradicate.

You feel humiliated. A mumbling mess of saltwater and nerves. You feel like you failed, even if this wasn't a test. You sat there and listened intently to the things you already knew but couldn't seem to follow. You pushed those words within you, but you'd always been so stubborn. It is your trait; you've always been told since you were a little girl. You are your own worst enemy.

You are cunning and ruthless to yourself; you can allow some kind of hope to bloom in your chest, but you can squash all of that in one blow.

You feel small, like you've been talked down to when you've always thought of your thoughts as superior. You are your own master; nobody tells you who you are and who you are not, what you fear, and why it is so.

And yet you were there, in the chair, knowing you'd submitted yourself to it because you were no longer in control of the havoc you yourself stirred.

You are hosting a revolution, and you know that, once again, you are in danger of destruction. You are rooting for the good to win, to release from the turmoil that you have been dreading—while resisting it with the devils you have acquainted yourself with. You are mad, switching back and forth, wanting to be better but loathing the trials you have to endure.

You have no one to blame. You want to blame everyone, the people who did this to you, the people who hurt you. She told you, "You can only control what you can now."

You are a swirl of emotions, your body collateral damage from the battle inside your head. You are bedbound and supine, unable to speak. You are weak. She told you, "You are so strong for holding on to this." She said it with such conviction that you wished to brandish the words into your own skin, make a scar out of them.

Your body is the land pillaged, raped, and harrowed by your own destructive thoughts. You have to have the same conviction, then recoup and reclaim the land that is yours, wish it no harm, and let it return to what it once was.

You have to learn how to be gentle. Your hands are calloused, and sometimes your desire to fix yourself comes with such a brute force that you end up hurting yourself more.

You need to return. Keep asking for counsel because you are lost in your own thoughts. Admission, that's the first step. Acceptance is next.

80

She feels like a fraud writing these words.
She is no more or less than the person reading this,
hoping to see the light between the cracks
to keep her afloat.

She is drowning in her own moat,
standing before her kingdom,
waiting to be conquered
to fill in her throne.

She feels unworthy of the love
and the praise perched at her door.
She is a fraud.
And yet—

She has the keys to the chambers.
She has always been who she said she was.
She was just challenged
and afraid of the war.

81

Mother, here are your children.
Two faces of depression:
one who fought the darkness
with the dark,
the other barely clutching on
to some kind of light.
Both valid,
both at the mercy of the demons
living in their minds.
You don't have to compare
and think of them as weak,
poke at the holes of their
lifeboats just to see.
None of this is your fault,
and don't despair over what
you could have done before.
Your children are still here,
and they need you—
not just the one,
always, both.

82

At this rate she's just working to pay for medical fees, and her hobbies include sitting in hospitals and private clinics' lobbies, driving to appointments, buying medicine, ninja crying in public. Sometimes it works; sometimes it still feels like she is a flinch away from breaking while everyone watches her spill her guts. She's on the streets screaming for medicine, for a better feeling, to be anything—but this.

83

Remember when we were young and you took me on a bike ride? I sat in front, holding on to the handlebars while you pedaled, and you told me, "Lead the way." It was scorching hot as I watched versions of us in black-and-white on the concrete—but that was my mistake. You told me to look up just about the time we hit the light post and we crashed. We both fell down and acquired scratches and bruises.

You never said it was my fault, but I could tell that you thought it.

We walked home, and we never rode the bike that way again. We never truly did things together anymore. I kept thinking that maybe if we'd tried again then, I would have paid much better attention, and we would have found a better sync.

These days, I still see you pedaling without direction, a man on a unicycle craning his neck for which way to go, but you don't know. You pedal in place, and you run out of air, and for the longest time, I thought this was just how you were.

I kept missing your SOS. I thought you liked staying in place, waiting for someone with the handlebars to lead you on.

I've got the handlebars from our childhood chained to my wrists as placement for my guilt, 'cause the last time we did this, we crashed on the floor.

I rang the bells to call for help, because now I know: good intentions are not always enough to save someone.

84

The more I look at you,
the more I see
the similarity—
only you're not him.
You didn't know me.

I wish you did.
I wish you had our history:
the years,
the longing,
the wanting.

I wish you were him in a brand-new body.

I'm cheating on a clean slate,
a second chance.
I just couldn't get it.

You're brand new for me,
but your face holds a memory.
Your soul is still a mystery;
I wish I knew you
and you knew me.

85

Maybe for a change
let's assume that this ends well.
Would you take the chance?

— *leap of faith*

86

Last week, you came to me,
not in a form of a dream or a memory.

It was really you,
all skin and bone
and a heart, still beating.

Funny, I thought I heard my name in between the rhythm.

87

If I told you how many times you've visited my dreams in all these years, you would think—no, you would know—how much you lived in me, despite living your life without me.

88

I remember your heart being so soft.
I must have bruised it with my
careless hands
once or twice—
or more; I never found out.

You said you didn't keep count.
Instead, I watched your heart turn hard.

I washed my hands clean,
but they had always been
stained red.

Yours or mine,
blood looked the same.

I remember your heart being soft.
My hands tried to handle
something so fragile,
maybe too late.
Maybe too soon.

89

You said, "It's us," like this was in a conversation we're still having. Like we didn't try to end things. Like we didn't run away from each other when the situation asked for at least one of us to show up. You said, "It's us," like it was an excuse for all the things that happened between us, the hurt we caused, and the time we wasted being apart.

You, me, in continents drifting apart, and you just said, "It's us," like the plates would move back and bring us together: a constant, inevitable thing. Not a memory, not forgotten.

When we met, I never thought that we would come to this. I had hoped that we would never have to reach the place where we expected hurt from each other, then used our love as an excuse for it.

90

And if you're gonna leave again,
don't even think about
coming back.

My life can't be a series
of recovering from your
calculated attacks.

91

You've visited me long enough that you are no longer a tourist.

92

She wrote love stories
but couldn't finish them all.
Only how they end.

— *happily ever after*

93

You say happy ever afters are not realistic only because you are afraid that women would believe it, and if they do, they would not settle for the bare minimum that you give.

You hate on the women who choose to believe that there is something better because you could not and would not be it.

— *on happy ever afters*

94

It's not gonna happen
all at once.
It's going to unravel
in the most beautiful way,
if you could just
stick around.

95

And what if the evil stepmother wasn't evil after all? What if she was just a woman who felt jealous? Because who hasn't, at least once in their lives, felt an ounce of it every time a young girl comes into a room with all of her naivety?

What if she was just a woman who wished she could have that again, the blinding protection of "what you don't know can't hurt you"? What if she wished for a moment to be who she was before, not this person who has weathered hurricanes, earthquakes, and the drought that is fast approaching her?

Maybe she missed the spring, and she recognized that young girls don't always see it when it is happening. They are always too busy wishing for a life that is far away from what they have at that very moment, not knowing that this will never be anymore.

What if she wasn't evil but just a woman who was in the middle of a fall, waiting for her leaves to shed so she could blossom once more?

96

These are her sore spots:

The word "weak,"
how that bruises her.
Green and yellow,
black and blue,
different hues.

His presence,
how he asks anyone she knows.
Seems like he didn't get the memo:
she doesn't want fake conversations anymore.

She's not thirteen.
She has stopped waiting for phone calls.
And if he did it now,
she already knows.

He taught her about spaces, distance—
if only he could respect hers.
She's grown up without him,
made her choice when she learned:

Blood isn't what makes a family.
Love is.

97

Some days you unfold;
some days you tuck yourself
back into your cocoon.

98

Sometimes you feel the weight
of another person's love
sink you further.

The expectations,
the responsibility of being loved—
you're not sure
you were built for that.

To love is to be accountable,
and when it gets bad,
you want all strings snapped.

But you have been looking
at love the wrong way.
It is not a stone
that sinks you down.

Love is the anchor
that grounds you
when you drift off lost.

99

There's power in speaking
the words that carried you through,
but there is joy,
so much joy,
in singing them, too.

There is life in the hum,
in the melody,
in every tremble of your
voice,
and in every syllable.

There is the music,
and then there is you.

100

Give yourself the gift of hindsight,
to be able to look back
at a difficult time
without panic,
to speak of a difficult feeling
without the fear of speaking it.

Give yourself the chance
to look down at the labyrinth
that you coursed through,
not to tell yourself
what you did wrong
but to embrace
what you've gone through.

101

And then there is Lorne,
with its strip of stores,
coffee shops, and galleries,
takeaway Chinese:
dumplings the size of
an infant's fist.

Young people meeting
on the streets,
adults in between breaks
getting a cuppa,
blowing rings.

Pedestrian lanes
heading to different directions,
streetlights blinking,
buskers getting your attention.

When I think of Lorne,
I make a silent hum.
My lips turn, and I envision:
home.

102

I like it here.
I am mostly worried about
where to go,
what to eat for lunch or so.

Sometimes I still think
about the things that worry me so,
but time moves differently here:
fast yet abundant.

The cold air sweeps me off my feet,
but there is sunlight.

Always sunlight.

103

Crimson,
the color of your shame
for wanting to change
where you stay.

Blue,
how it runs through you,
unable to recognize
the country you once knew.

Three stars
and a sun,
wherever you could wish upon.
You love your country—you do.
But you no longer feel alive
in a place that was once home to you.

104

Settling—
not accepting what is at hand,
never what you really want—
but *s e t t l i n g*:
setting down roots,
satisfied.

105

There will be thunder.
You will shiver in the cold.
But the clouds will roll.

— *The sun will return*

106

They're playing our song;
I don't feel the need to call
you, out of nowhere.

— *moving on*

107

I will replace your name with a new meaning,
stop banning it from existence.
No more a syllable that shouldn't pass my lips,
I will speak your name and deem it
no longer a word that hurts,
no longer a memory that haunts.
I will give your name a better feeling,
my own version of a happy ending.

108

You know when we were young and people asked, "Where do you go for vacations? Are you a city person? Or do you enjoy the outdoors more?" It took me years of traveling to learn that I like cities. I like shops. I like places to get books, coffee, food. Places to see art. Study art. I like traveling in between: observing, studying, seeing people in their day-to-day while I am on pause and at rest. I like being a tourist pretending to be one with the crowd.

But then, I've also started to crave the slow life: the charm of small towns, the little shops, handmade things, local artists, odd histories. Small things that are *their* big things.

The quiet life.

The simple dream.

Contentment.

Maybe that's what I've always been seeking.

109

She's already lived
a thousand lives,
seen enough places
to come back around,
met people old and new,
played a different role or two.

Then she comes home
to solitude.

Home is wherever she goes,
whatever she decides it to be.
She belongs to herself
and to whoever she chooses fit.

ACKNOWLEDGMENTS

with love and gratitude to

My constants:
Layla Tanjutco, best editor
Reginald Lapid, best and most patient cover designer
#romanceclass community for the motivation and inspiration,
   always

KB Meniado, best beta reader!
Cheyenne Raine
Raine Sarmiento
Sheila, for the nitty gritty
Patty Rice and the Andrews McMeel Publishing team for
   creating book number four with me.
Maan and Jay, for the trips and happy things.
B and Kara, for the safe space.
Tita Thelma, who is missed.
Family and friends, in real life and in fandom,
the cities that became my shelter,
and the people who had been my home,

Babalik ako.
Mahal ko kayo.

ABOUT THE AUTHOR

Dawn Lanuza writes contemporary romance, young adult fiction, and poetry. She has two first loves—music and writing—and is lucky enough to surround herself with them. She started to self-publish in 2014 with her debut romance novel, *The Boyfriend Backtrack,* and then proceeded to write two more books. In 2016, she self-published her first poetry collection, *The Last Time I'll Write About You,* which debuted at number one on Amazon's Hot New Releases and has stayed on its bestsellers chart for over a year, before it was rereleased as an expanded and revised edition by Andrews McMeel Publishing. She has been traveling in and out of her country, the Philippines, to find the next place to call home.

You may contact her at:

hello@dawnlanuza.com

www.dawnlanuza.com

Andrews McMeel Publishing
a division of Andrews McMeel Universal
1130 Walnut Street, Kansas City, Missouri 64106

www.andrewsmcmeel.com

Cover and interior illustration by Raine Sarmiento
Illustrator's model: Iris Dijkers
Cover art design by Reginald Lapid

21 22 23 24 25 BVG 10 9 8 7 6 5 4 3 2 1

ISBN: 978-1-5248-6181-0

Library of Congress Control Number: 2020940641

Editor: Patty Rice
Art Director/Designer: Holly Swayne
Production Editor: Elizabeth A. Garcia
Production Manager: Carol Coe

ATTENTION: SCHOOLS AND BUSINESSES
Andrews McMeel books are available at quantity discounts with bulk purchase for educational, business, or sales promotional use. For information, please e-mail the Andrews McMeel Publishing Special Sales Department: specialsales@amuniversal.com.